Knausz Erzsébet

Contemporary Methods in Teaching Speaking

Knausz Erzsébet

Contemporary Methods in Teaching Speaking

VDM Verlag Dr. Müller

Imprint

Bibliographic information by the German National Library: The German National Library lists this publication at the German National Bibliography; detailed bibliographic information is available on the Internet at http://dnb.d-nb.de.

Any brand names and product names mentioned in this book are subject to trademark, brand or patent protection and are trademarks or registered trademarks of their respective holders. The use of brand names, product names, common names, trade names, product descriptions etc. even without a particular marking in this works is in no way to be construed to mean that such names may be regarded as unrestricted in respect of trademark and brand protection legislation and could thus be used by anyone.

Cover image: www.purestockx.com

Publisher:
VDM Verlag Dr. Müller Aktiengesellschaft & Co. KG, Dudweiler Landstr. 125 a, 66123 Saarbrücken, Germany,
Phone +49 681 9100-698, Fax +49 681 9100-988,
Email: info@vdm-verlag.de

Copyright © 2008 VDM Verlag Dr. Müller Aktiengesellschaft & Co. KG and licensors
All rights reserved. Saarbrücken 2008

Produced in USA and UK by:
Lightning Source Inc., La Vergne, Tennessee, USA
Lightning Source UK Ltd., Milton Keynes, UK
BookSurge LLC, 5341 Dorchester Road, Suite 16, North Charleston, SC 29418, USA

ISBN: 978-3-639-01730-4

CONTENT

Preface
1. An introduction to the topic 2

1.1. General remarks on speaking 2

1.2 The role of speaking in the history of language pedagogy 2
1.2.1. Speaking in the best-known methods:
Including GT, SM, AL, AV 5
1.2.2. Speaking in the XX. Century 5
1.2.2.1. The humanist approaches 6
1.2.2.2. The communicative language teaching 7

2. Attitudes to learning and teaching speaking 9

2.1. The factors helping and paralysing the development of Students' speaking skills 9
2.1.1. Problems with communicative competence 9
2.1.2. The role of motivation 10
2.1.3. Language anxiety 11
2.1.4. Students' personality 12
2.1.4.1. Extrovert/Introvert types of personality 12
2.1.4.2. Self-confidence and inhibition 12

2.2. The teacher: devices for creating the most comfortable atmosphere for students' progress in speaking 13
2.2.1 Teachers' personality and their attitude to teaching 13
2.2.2. Classroom solutions 15
2.2.3. Using audio-visual aids 16
2.2.4. Using drama techniques 18
2.2.5. Project work 20

3. Current attitudes to learning and teaching speaking in everyday life realisation: A survey 21

3.1. Some introductiory remarks 21

3.2. Speaking skill from the point of view of the teachers and the students (The analysis of the questionnaires) 21

3.3. The effect of drama techniques concerning human factors: A role play in the classroom (An experiment) 25

4. Final remarks 31

Preface

During my university studies I was given plenty of information and I was to choose the pieces I thought I would use in teaching.

Remembering the difficult points I used to have to cope with during learning English, one of them was speaking, I consciously paid attention to find a good or in some cases better solution than my teachers used to have. It is very important to look back and learn from the ancestors, so firstly, I intended to give a brief summary of how the classical methods treated speaking.

To speak in the target language may not always be easy for students; they may be paralysed when they have to do so. Based on my experience and observations I am trying to highlight some factors, which may cause problems for students such as language anxiety or even, their personality.

To help students defeat these problems, teachers can do a lot. In the second part of the same chapter, I am attempting to give some possible solutions. During the university years, teacher trainees study pedagogy and methodology in theory but it is interesting to see these things in reality, as well. In the third part, I asked teachers and students about the relevant topics of my thesis. Having dealt with drama pedagogy, also in theory, I did a role- play with two groups, an adult and a teenage one to see people' reaction to this quite unknown field in Hungarian schools.

To sum up, my work is to present all I have learnt and experienced during my university studies and my teaching practise period. I hope you will find it interesting and maybe given thought and ideas from it.

1. An introduction to the topic

1.1 General remarks on speaking

Speaking is one of the four basic skills. Skill is „a hierarchy of decisions and automated actions used as an integrated whole, the lower ones depending higher ones." (Bygate M. 1978:116) Skills can be classified as active or passive, ones sound-centred/auditive or letter-centred/visual skills. Reading and listening are the passive ones; they are for comprehension; and speaking with writing are the active ones used mainly for communication.

According to a newer classification, however the four basic skills – listening, reading, speech and writing – are said to be „simple skills", while interpretation and translation are „complex skills" because there two languages are involved.

1. 2. The role of speaking in the history of language pedagogy

1.2.1. Speaking in the best-known methods: the Grammar Translation, the Direct Method, the Audiolingual and Audio-Visual Methods

Speaking as a skill was neglected in the classical methods for a long time, although it had been highly respected by the Greek and the Romans. The end of the 19th century brought crucial change when new fields of science started to develop and as a result, linguistic (both descriptive and historical) and phonetics emerged. This had a huge effect on linguistic methodology. That time it was the Grammar Translation Method, which was used extensively. This way of teaching a foreign language, however, completely ignored speaking. Authentic, mainly literary texts were used for translation and explanation of the different grammar items. The lessons were held in the mother tongue not in the target language. In spite of all its advantages, it is a rather exhausting method for learners: they are expected to study texts by heart and the memorisation of the plenty of information, declinations, that is actually rote learning, are also very tiring.

As the International Phonetics Association (IPA) was founded in 1896, by the end of the 19th century, the need for speech was getting more and more strong, as well, thus a demand for change was urged. The result of this revolt was the Direct Method (DM), which fulfilled the need of prompt communication. (Bárdos J, 2000: 181)

This new way is the complete opposition of the previous one in every field. Authentic texts were replaced with the ones on customs, geography, history. Speech became the centre of teaching, then reading and writing in the end. Not to mention the great numbers of realia which the Grammar Translation method completely put off, as well as mimes and gestures. According to one of the founders Berlitz, only native speakers should teach, and helped students to practise the language this way. His 12 point pieces of advice became the base by the method and describes the difference between the Grammar-Translation and the Direct Method:

- never speak: demonstrate
- never explain: act
- never make a speech: ask questions
- never imitate mistakes: correct
- never speak with single words: use sentences
- never speak too much: make students speak much
- never use the book: use your lesson plan
- never jump around: follow your plan
- never go too fast: keep the pace of the students
- never speak too slowly: speak normally
- never speak too loudly: speak normally
- never be impatient: take it easy

With the development of the equipment used in language teaching and the emerging new fields: psychology and linguistics which turned to the structuralism, a new way of thinking was formed which was the Audiolingual Method. As for the former fact, tapes, recorders were perfected – two-track recordery started to spread in the 40s-50s, where both the student's and the teacher's voice could be recorded, and in the 60s, polyester tapes began to be used. Two basic types of language labs were developed: the AA (audio-action) and AAC (audio –active comparative). The main difference between the two is that only the second one could record the student's voice, as well. (Bárdos J, 1988: 83) The advantage of involving language labs into language teaching is that this method could differentiate as well as individualize, helped this way the students to develop in their pace.

Language teachers got more and more interested in the scientific researches; from psychology, for instance the behaviorism, from linguistics, the structuralism had great impact on language pedagogy.

Based on the experience of the DM, Fries, Pike and Lado worked a new method out. (Bárdos J, 1988: 80) Here, speech and communication kept its importance, but according to the structuralist view, language was separated into very small pieces so that the whole could be rebuilt again.

The Audiolingual Method separated the four basic skills on purpose and emphasised that speaking and listening are the basic ones; the other two (reading and writing) were, however, not ignored, either. (Bárdos J, 1988: 91)

Pattern drills were used to make students memorize the basic patterns of the language. The main principle of the method is the repetition and imitation, which help plenty of people in language learning, but on one hand, long and lifeless dialogues may later be found boring and secondly, one cannot condition all utterances for lifelong. In one word, the method lacks the interaction skills.

As the Audiovisual Method does not consider the explanation of grammar important and writing and reading, are put off, it may seem to return to the Direct Method. On the other hand, it uses grammar drills, although they are not meaningful. (Bárdos J, 1988; 95) The whole process starts out from sight and ends in the grammar segments. Plenty of pictures, realia are used: sketches, cartoons, flashcards, slides, motion pictures. This method is very vivid, entertaining but uses too rigid and strict teaching sequences (do this in 5 minutes, that in 20 minutes etc). In spite of this, it is situation-based, i.e. students are given social context and can try themselves out in meaningful communication.

1.2.2 Speaking in the 20th century

By 1970s-80s great changes could be felt in language pedagogy. There were two main branches among the methods. The first group was based on a psyhologycal view which said that students are complete personalities who gain a lot to themselves by language learning. While the second one, the communicative view, put functions into the centre instead of studying the code, the grammatical forms, notions of a foreign language.

1.2.2.1 The humanistic approaches: CLL,TPR, SW, SU

The humanistic approaches emerged in the 1970s in the U.S.A. 'As opposed to the traditional view of education where the curriculum was in the focus, the humansitic approach concentrates on the learner and her attitudes and experiences, thus trying to construct her curriculum not solely by the teacher, but with the cooperation of the learner, the teacher and other stakeholders (parents, admininstrators). The teacher is more commonly referred to as facilitator of learning, indicating the flexibility and intimacy of education.'(Csoma K., 2003)

The following language teaching approaches developed based on humanism:

A. Community Language learning (CLL)

The method was created by Charles Curran. ' The basic idea behind (it) is that the language learner is treated as a client or patient, and the teacher behaves like a counsellor helping to repair problems.'(Csoma K., 2003).

Students sit in circle and do exercises in the target language. The teacher is a complete outsider, never corrects mistakes. If a problem arises, she helps students but just whispers so as not to disturb the others.

The lessons are tape-recorded for the aim of learning this way, as well.

The whole method is based on a very intimate relationship between the teacher, 'the counsellor' and the student, 'the client'.

B. Total Physical Response (TPR)

The founder of this approach is James Asher. It is '…a language learning method based on the coordination of speech and action'. (Csoma K.,2003) The method uses body movements or 'kinesthetic' situations to place matter into long-term memory.'(Csoma K,2003).

It is mainly used in early stages of language learning and its application is limited as there is a range of vocabulary and grammar items which can not easily be introduced by only motions.

C. The Silent Way (SW)

The method was founded by Galeb Gattegno in 1972. He thought that the essence of language learning is students' self-discovery and what is only needed are mime and gestures, or visual aids and the so-called 'Cuisiniere-rod' (sets of rods of different lengths and colours).

'During this process, the teacher remains relatively silent, the aim being to encourage the student of the language to be increasingly self-reliant and independent from the teacher. The teacher guides the whole process but by saying as little as possible. Learners have to learn how to test for themselves their hypothesis about how the target language works.' (Csoma K., 2003).

D. Suggestopedia (SU)

According to the founder of the method, Georgi Lozanov (1978), '…as we get older we accept social norms and adjust our personalities to conform to them.'(Csoma K.,2003).

In adulthood, we lose capabilities we used as a child, and the chief principle in language learning is to turn back to this self. The way of going back to it is via 'suggestion', relaxed alertness.

He concentrated on usable skills; he considered real-life-like situations.

'… extended dialogues, often several pages in length, in role-play format (…) accompanied by vocabulary list and observations on grammatical points.'

First, the teacher reads the text aloud to accompaniment of music. Then, the monologue or dialogue is performed and in the end students have to re-produce it.

1. 2. 2. 2. The Communicative Language Learning

In the 1980s, the attention was diverted to the process of speech from the language itself in language pedagogy.

Different concepts like „**appropriateness**" and „**acceptability**", and '**communication competence**' come into being and were determined. *Acceptability* relates to whether a phrase or sentence is grammatically and semantically acceptable to a native speaker. Appropriacy in the expectation that various language styles are used depending on various situations and the chosen linguistic devices should match the given formal or informal setting. (Kurtán Zs., 1999: 73)

The concepts above are corrected in the **language norm**, which is the balance between the two: a dynamic compromise between linguistic codification and social convention.

It was defined that there is a distinction between a person's knowledge of language (Kurtán Zs, 1999: 75) that is **linguistic competence** and the use of it that is the **linguistic performance.** (Noam Chomoky's terms; Aspects of the Theory of Syntax)

According to the Canal & Swain model the communicative competence requires the following factors:

1. **Linguistic competence** (mentioned before) which means fluency and accurancy.

2. **Sociolinguistic competence** that is proper language norm (acceptability and appropriateness – defined above).

3. **Discourse competence** which requires the skill of producing larger pieces of texts both in speech and writing. Cohesion that is „the grammatical and/or lexical relationships between different sentences or between different parts of a sentence" (Kurtán Zs, 1999: 89) and coherence, „the relationships which links the meanings of utterances in a discourse or of the sentences in a text" (Kurtán Zs, 1999: 90) should also be mentioned here.

4. **The strategic competence** which is in fact different kinds of avoidance techniques. It becomes very important when there is problem with the first three. Those who do not have strategic competence, commit a mistake.

It was also realised that it is not enough to teach students different grammatical items, it is also significant to make them accustomed to the fact that the grammatical realisation of a sentence may have different meanings, as well.

Several researchers, such as Wittgenstein, Searle, Gumperz, Hassau and Hymes started studying the communicative functions: **Austin**, for instance, defined his theory where the actual form of the message, is „*locution*". The next step in the process is „*illocution*", i.e. what you implied with what you said. For instance, let's have a situation. The phone is ringing and John is having a bath. He is shouting out of the bathroom: „I'm in the bath!". The sentence „I'm in the bath" can have different meanings. Providing we do not know the context, it can be said that it is a simple statement, but put it into the situation, it is more possible that he wants his wife to answer the phone. The phenomenon of expressing such hidden meanings is called 'illocution'.

The third and last part of Austin's theory is „*perlocution*" which is the actual event on the other speaker made by the utterance. In our example, It is John's wife who answers the phone. This theory is called **„Speech Act Theory"** which should be very important to make students familiar with since this may help students see the language in context, not only just the separate parts of it (such as vocabulary, grammar).

2. Attitudes to learning and teaching speaking

It is often said that the 21st century is the era of information, which requires proper communication. It is of increasing significance to teach children foreign languages but unfortunately, in Hungary there are few of them who can use their knowledge in everyday situations, too. To achieve communication competence, it is not enough to study the rules of grammar and the vocabulary (=to gain linguistic competence). During the lessons students should be given the opportunity to use the language in real-life situations. Most of them are unable to use the language during a holiday for example, although she/he has good mark in the target language.

What can be the reasons why students are unable to speak and what solutions may be done? In this part, to find a possible answer to these questions is attempted.

2.1 The factors helping and paralysing the development of students' speaking skills

2.1.1. Problems with the communicative competence

There can be several factors why students do not like speaking. When studying speaking as a skill, Bygate (1978) states that the basic thing is for students to use their oral skill is to thoroughly know grammar and vocabulary. He says that „there is a difference between knowledge about a language and skill in using it. We do not merely know how to assemble sentences in the abstract: we have to produce them and adapt them to the circumstances." (Bygate M, 1978: 3) This means continuent decision making while speaking. Students should be trained for the situations when they have problems with firstly grammar. Their strategic competence should be improved: i.e. they should be able to tell their intended message in different ways. Of course, it can only be fully expected on higher level but teachers should arouse students' attention to certain connections at their level.

Secondly, in case their vocabulary is poor and the necessary word does not come into their mind, they can describe it as well. As for me, students usually became frightened in such situations instead of thinking. Students should be encouraged to use their common sense. They are constantly afraid of making mistakes while speaking and, this misleads the attention to something more important: the joy of speaking in a foreign language. Of course, it is very significant to speak with as correct grammar as one can but nowadays most of the children can only see the parts of the language and consider studying grammar and vocabulary boring. Thus the intended aim of learning the language i.e. to be able to communicate tends to be fade. This way they lose their motivation and the learning process its effectiveness.

2.1.2. The role of motivation

Motivation '… is a constraint generated by a stimulus or an emotion. The constraint always ends in activity and can be connected to a certain situation or exercise but may also be a general kind.' (Bárdos J, 2000: 242).

There may be plenty of reasons why people start learning a language.

Ansubel is his theory on education (Ansubel, 1968: 368) describes six layers of motivation. They are the following: curiosity, desire for manipulation i.e. changing things, encouragement and desire for knowledge and self-realization.

In case, their curiosity and desire for knowledge is at high rate, their motivation is called **'integrative or intrinsic'**, according to the classification of Gardner and Lambert (1972). **'Instrumental or extrinsic'** motivation is when somebody is interested in language learning only for the reason of its benefits, for example, knowing a language is requested for a job, or for somebody's degree. (Bárdos J, 2000: 244).

There are a great number of factors which might have an effect how students are motivated in the target language. Especially, it is the subject material that counts but a poorly furnished or organised classroom can reduce students' interest.

According to Dörnyei (1994) students are the most sensitive about the material, the teacher's activity and the fellow members of the group. (BárdosJ, 2000: 244).

Nowadays, a new sort of motivation is tending to turn up which Bárdos (2000) calls **'recreational motivation'**. Having spread the Internet recently more and more people are getting interested in language learning on entertaining and cultural purposes.

Teachers should assist keeping these, in most of the cases, instinct –based motivations in students and reinforced them with conscious motivative strategies. (Bárdos J, 2000: 244).

2.1.3. Language anxiety

Researchers started dealing with this phenomenon in the 70s although it has been present in classrooms since foreign languages were begun to teach.

Language anxiety usually appears when one uses a language s/he has not reached an appropriate level. (BárdosJ, 2000: 246).

According to Anna Turula (2000), the factors behind this phenomenon can be – beyond students' personality, the learning environments, including the classroom itself, the interaction between the groupmates.

Fears of being given negative judgements in front of the whole class or occasionally, the teachers' incorrect reaction to an answer, for instance, maybe paralysing force for students.

Bárdos (2000) indicates that dreads of communication and also assessment belong to the same category.

It is natural that those who suffer from language anxiety try to get rid of it. When attempting to cease these unpleasant feeling in students, Bárdos (2000) says that students tend to behave in two ways. There are ones with the so-called *mature and unmature defending systems*.

Those, belonging to the first group, are able to accept the differences between the two languages; they have empathy, they are able to foresee the difficulties and may try to use their sense of humour instead of being depressed; they never give up.

The latter group is unable to come up with the ambiguities; they usually see the situation in one way and show unwillingness to change their minds. (See Appendix I.)

And here, the problem of extrovert/introvert personalities and the question of openness and closeness emerge. When students come across a problematic area of the target language, it is not rare that they promptly lose their temper. At this point a teacher has to become a psychologist, and with her patience and clear arguments she should make the mature defending strategies in students start. This is not easy but significant because according to MacIntyre and Gardner (1991), language anxiety is a learned reaction which only come round when students have several times had negative experiences in connection with the target language. (Bárdos J, 2000: 247).

Language anxiety is rather different from other kinds of stresses but it is essential to pay attention to it as it may affect students' performance and they become undermotivated.

And if so, this leads to exaggerated anxiety and because of the level of which students may be discouraged themselves from language learning.

2.1.4. Students' personality

2.1.4.1. Extrovert and introvert types of personality

Connected to language anxiety, the problem with extro- and intorvert personalities has been mentioned. It was Jung who introduced these concepts. The distinction between the two originated from the question whether the inner force of the personality is targeted at its inner or outer world. Jung distinguishes them on the basis of whether the people in these categories function on emotional- experimental or instinctive terms. He made distinction between the group of people making decisions with the help of intellectual processes or basically, with the help of emotions.

Extrovert personalities are highly interested in the outer world which gives energy to them. They need to be received constant feedback from outside, which enables them to express their feelings and it is also the demand for their self-fulfilment. (Bárdos J, 2000: 250).

Mysers-Briggs worked on the description of different personal features using Jung's classification and they said that the introvert have limited relationships although their way of thinking is very deep. They usually keep their energies and they tend to turn to their own inner world. They have a good sense of concentration, too. (Bárdos J, 2000: 251).

2.1.4.2. Self-confidence and inhibition

Self-confidence is closely connected to self-image that is built up from three components. *The Impression*, we create about ourselves; *the ideal Self-image*, we intend to become; *the Self-esteem*, which expresses the values of the personality we believe we have. Providing that there is huge gap between the ideal and the real self-image, then it leads to uncertainty, inhibitedness and it can be extremely harmful in developing the students' speaking skills. They become paralysed and do not use all the opportunities to speak in the target language.

However,"…'the home feeling' can encourage the shy students to attempt speaking; developing such atmosphere is as essential a task for teachers as selecting the proper subject material."(Bárdos J, 2000: 245).

The desire in some students to be centre figure in the lesson generated by exaggerated self-confidence, can cause unexpected problems teachers should be ready to cope with.

It is essential to find the best methods so as to be able to provide suitable language practice for both the shy and the confident students.

'The most satisfactory the situation is when the difference between the ideal and real self-image is very slight.'(Bárdos J, 2000: 245).

2.2. The teacher: devices for creating the most comfortable atmosphere for students' progress in speaking

2.2.1. Teachers' personality and their attitude to teaching

'Teachers open the door …and you enter by yourself'.

When being in a language lesson, most of the students may lose their self-consciousness, as they feel not sure he solutions and the answers. They usually come from rather different circumstances and they also have very different rate of knowledge. Having a brief look at the history of language methodology, we can see that at the beginning the language itself was considered to be only a system and aim. The source of learning was the teacher and the material. The last century's reforms changed the situation: students became more and more the main factors of the language learning process, which view was later extended in the 20th century's communicative and humanistic approaches having discussed. (Poór Z, 2001: 97).

A teacher should be in the middle of the group, s/he is a centre figure in the sense that s/he should start building a group up from the people who are strangers to one another in the classroom at the beginning of a course. In the learning process teachers should be behind, letting students in the foreground as what is of most significance here is the students' development. But when speaking about teachers as the linking force of the group, they have definitely to be in the centre. They should have special skills of communication.

A relaxed atmosphere should be created where students can feel safety and warmth. They should feel that they are allowed to make mistakes, even errors, because this is the place, the classroom, the group, that is there to help them stand up from the fall. This is the place where all the unclear things can be discussed and because of the possible mistakes one is not punished or made fun of. Students should understand that the language learning process is first of all for improving their competence as well as for their personal development. All in all they should see what is happening to them and for them is their learning. (Poór Z, 2001:99) For reaching this level, teachers must be in good mental and physical health.

According to the humanist view, students have complete personality enriched by language learning. Thus, avoiding hurting this personality is surely important. Each student carries something special in himself and a teacher should look for it first, then try to lead the student's attention to that certain feature of his by which s/he is gifted. Or, in case, the student has no sense to language learning, a teacher should help him to be able to follow the pace of the others. Student and teacher have divided responsibility toward each other and they should create mutual trust with each other. In developing trust, teachers also have crucial importance.

The way I see it, for gaining students' belief in you, the first step is to make students feel that you are there to assist their language improvement, and not for the reason that you want to force them to learn the language at all cost. A very positive attitude to students where you message them that you accept them the way they are must be a very good solution. You should be authentic that is to keep to balance between experience and awareness. Teachers should talk to students more and the relationship between them should not be only restricted to the school matters. Of course, time is a determining factor and teachers are forced to keep the pace of the syllabus, thus there is no time or very little for talking. Unfortunately time is not only one of the restrictive forces. Although, sometimes it would be necessary for teachers to ask students why they have or have not done this or that, because there are cases when it is not the students' fault, but the circumstances', his family background or other reasons. It is very sad that nowadays very little attention is paid to these factors even if it is clearly known that students' current performance may be effected by plenty of causes beyond their control.

It does not mean that students never want to cheat, but teachers' empathy at the right time may make a lot for them.

There were plenty of researchers who tried to classify the different types of teachers. One of these, according to **Katz** (1996) is the following:

1. **Choreographer**: who always wants to plan everything for the students
2. **The Earth mother** would like to be trusted, told about everything, and is a real peace - maker.
3. **Entertainer**, who is artistic, s/he has understandable metaphors and good sense of humour.
4. **The professor** who concentrates on the subject material all the time

Striving for some features of the 2nd and 3rd one may be a rather good solution. It may be soothing for some students to know that their teacher can be relied on. The way to open the door leading to students' attention might be done by humour: *"make people laugh and you can tell them almost everything onward"* (anonymous) To laugh means that you are not tense but relaxed and this is the state especially needed for learning.

It has to be remarked, however, that teachers should keep an acceptable distance from students as well, because the growing relationship may cause discipline problems. Anna Turula (2002) summarises this: '... what we need is a collaborative spirit, a clear sense of direction and a sense of fun'.

2.2.2. Classroom solutions

There are students who may be more successful in overcoming their fears when they are not asked in front of the whole class. The proper classroom management can be a suitable force to make students comfort.(See Appendix III.)

Pair work

Pair work is present in language methodology for a long time. It is very useful because students are less anxious about their mistakes as they do not commit them before the whole class, just in front of one member.

This way of speaking practice might, however, become boring if students have always the same partner. A very creative solution of this problem is the following: the teacher holds some ribbons in his hand and each of the students takes one side of them. When all the students have one they smoothly pull the ribbons and the teacher lets them. Then students have to find their classmates at the other end of the ribbon, and that person is their partner in the lesson.

The other solution can be to prepare 3 or 4 stages in the classroom. The stages should follow the subject material, they may be for instance 'at the clothes shop', 'at the doctor's' etc., but they should be real life situation. Cards are waiting for students with the instructions what the have to buy, or what their illness is, for example. When they have acted the situation out, they go to another stage, and on and on.

Group work

According to **Brumfit** (1984) "small groups provide greater intensity of involvement, so that the quality of language practice is increased, and the opportunities for feedback and monitoring also, given adequate guidance and preparation by the teacher. The setting if more natural than that of the full class, for the size of the group resembles that of normal conversational groupings. Because of this, the stress which accompanies 'public' performance in the classroom should be reduced." (Bygate M., 1987:97)

The physical arrangement of the classroom

The physical arrangement of the classroom may help students to open themselves. Sitting in circle or U-shape might be preferable in language teaching than the conventional frontal one.

2.2.3. Using audio-visual aids

In the history of language methodology, the audio-visual demonstration in lessons was completely ignored by the Grammar Translation method. Not regarding the earlier intentions such as **Comenius'** Orbis Pictus, it was the Direct Method that first brought the need for this kind of demonstration. Using audiovisual aids usually aims at helping students comprehend the new language stimuli and this way they can see the new material in context. It is significant for students to be given understandable explanations because this way they feel like learning as they have more success. Even according to **Hill** (1990) a classroom furnished in the simplest way is the worst surrounding for learning a language, it is essential to have some ornaments in the classroom which helps students put into the context the target language demands. (Poór Z., 2001:28)

On the basis of this we can see that the basic function of the audio- visual devices is context creation. There are plenty of such devices that may be used and one of their advantages is that they can be suitable for all the stages of a lesson. According to **Janet McAlpin** (1980) a picture or photo, for instance, can be an aid of presentation when introducing new topics or presenting structures. They may be part of practice in drills or pair work, but other activities or skills, for example, reading, writing, can be transformed from them. Not to mention the fact that when seeing a picture, something comes into our mind (an old memory, another picture we saw somewhere, etc.) in one word we get an impression, and it helps us express our feelings and the picture may remind the students of something as well. "Experiments will familiarise not only you, but also your students, with the possibilities." (McAlpin J., 1980: 53). And when paying attention to developing speaking skills one of the most essential factors is to make students relaxed, which is easier when students are familiarised with the topics.

Having emphasised the role of context creation, pictures and photos offer endless opportunities in teaching. There are, however, other ways of making the lesson more interesting and understandable for students. Let's take the example of cards and different figures prepared beforehand. There is a model for explaining the comparison of adjectives. The three figures, Brian, Jack and Rachel are said to be friends. First, students have to observe their height and say sentences according to it. Then it is told to students that these three friends wanted to buy some books and went to two bookshops to see where the books are cheaper. Students are expected to compare the prices of the books in the two shops. This exercise was tried out among 15- year- old students, and they liked it very much. (See Appendix II).

Here pictures, photos and cards have been emphasised, but, of course, there are several other aids as well:

1. **Types of boards are the following:** blackboard with written chalk image; white board with written or drawn image; magnetic and flannel boards with other visuals on them.

    It is very useful to let students write or draw onto the board, it may makes them more motivated.

2. **Flashcards** with words, phrases, structures and sentences are also used.
3. **Projected images** such as slides, filmstrips, OHP (overhead projector), episcope images, motion pictures, projected video are also exciting to involve in the English lessons.
4. **Diorama, models, realia** are good soultions, too.

There is above all one, this summary should have been begun with, is the teacher himself. His gestures, mimes and body language play crucial role, too. In case he is a bit talented in acting, he may act out a story without words for students, and they can guess what is happening. A new topic can be introduced with pantomime.

Using audio-visual aids is extremely advantegous because they are very spectacular and attract students very much.

2.2.4. Using drama techniques

"I hear and I forget,

I listen and I remember,

I do and I understand."

(Chinese proverb)

One may think that using drama techniques have just been involved in language teaching recently. However, even **Comenius** said in Scola Ludus, Sárospatak (1636): "Everything that is happening in public is like theatre. That is the reason why those who will be involved in public life should be educated in a way that they will be enabled to completely fulfil their task."

Drama techniques aim at helping, building and forming the participants' personality as well as making the communication easier for foreign language learners. (Gabnai K., 1993:7)

Role-plays

There are three basic forms of role plays: situational role plays, simulations, drama games.

Role plays are the activities where students are expected to enter into the spirit of a given situation. Their task is to behave exactly the same way as the character formed by them would do. At the end of the play they will be enriched by the experience they have just gained about the character, or about themselves. A role play is a good opportunity for students to observe the different samples of behaviour of the environment as well as their own. (Poór Z.,2001:44)

Situational role plays

Situational role plays are excellent vehicles when we intend to make students accustomed to every day situations, as in this kind of role play students are asked to act out a situation can be found in reality. The characters they should form are existing ones.

Simulations

In simulations the environment of the game is unreal but to fulfil the task students have to depend on their own real experiences, although they are also given a fictive role, character. Thus it is the student who put himself into a social context. (Poór Z., 2001:44) "It is an excellent vehicle for developing students' discussion skills, but may also involve reading, listening, specific language structures and functions and particular areas of vocabulary. It may take a little time to set up a simulation, but once it is on the way students suddenly find themselves in a different world, and the experience is extremely enriching." (Porter Ladouse G., 1987:159)

Drama games

Students, who take part in drama games, undertake communicative exercises realised by strategies based on real life experiences. The character they are demanded to build up is fictive, as well as the given situation. (Poór Z., 2001:44)

Drama games can be used in two different ways. Firstly a tale, a short story or a play was adapted onto stage. It is usually connected to spare time activities. Later it was realised that these techniques – for example discussion of the features of the characters, analysing the situations, events in the play – can easily be lead to foreign language classrooms. (Poór Z., 1995:71)

Drama techniques provide prompt feedback for both the teacher and the students. It is an extremely student-centred process because it offers the possibility for them to express their hidden feelings and it also makes them free form the bounds of their personalities as after understanding the task, students can let themselves go and have fun while working most of the cases.

Having mentioned that students can see plenty of different samples of behaviour. According to **Medgyes** (1986) role plays "...bring the outside world closer to the so called 'classroom world'" (Poór Z., 1995:41)

Role plays in foreign languages help students to be used to using the language fluently, by which the interactions among the group members can be increased. (Poór Z., 1995:41)

As Alan Maley wrote: "I believe in it (drama) because it changes my students from a 'room full of strangers' into a happy, cohesive group. I believe in it because it makes the whole process of learning a language a richly creative and fulfilling experience. I believe in it because it works." (Maley, A., 1987:133)

2.2.5. Project work

The project work as a process has roots in pragmatism according to which the essence of life is activity. '... the target of teaching is the education in the light of enabling students to do everything that they have opportunity of and to take as much experience as they can. (Takács L., 1996: 98).

In accordance with this, the project work is a series of activities that is planned by the teacher and the students together. This is not only for developing language skills, but it also offers opportunities for practising the skills essential for communication in a foreign language and not at least for establishing possibility for students to fulfil their personalities.

During the project work students are working on creating the product which has real function in real life. This product is called 'the project'.

The main point is that while working students co-operate with one another. It can be seen from the above facts that this method is quite student-centred. The chief aim is by exploiting the subject material that makes it possible for students to fulfil and understand their own personalities. The project work is targeted at topics, and not at specific language usage.

3. Current attitudes to learning and teaching speaking in everyday realisation: a survey

3. 1. Some introductory remarks

There is plenty of reference available in language pedagogy and a great number of researches have been prepared on teaching speaking so far but the participants involved in the learning process, the teachers and the students have rarely been asked about their opinion on this matter.

The following survey aim at inquiring about firstly, teachers' methods on improving students' speaking skills, secondly on students' present level of the same skill and their demands for developing it, and thirdly, the survey is attempting to study the effectiveness of role plays.

3.2 Speaking skills from the point of view of the teachers and the students (The analysis of the questionnaires)

<u>Introduction</u>

In the first part of the survey 122 (68 males and 54 females) students and their teachers (13) were asked. The survey was taken in the following schools: Baross Gábor Secondary School of Economics, Deák Ferenc Secondary School of Economics, Móra Ferenc Primary and Secondary Grammar School in Győr and Thuri György Secondary Grammar School in Várpalota. The age of the questioned students varies between 14 and 17 years.

An adult group was also inquired; their age is between 18 and 40. All the questioned persons are at about basic level. The questionnaires had been prepared in Hungarian so as to avoid language difficulties. (See Appendix IV.)

The objective was to be given answers to the following questions:

1) Whether students feel they can use the target language in every day situations based on their current level.

2) As for speaking, how they feel when being asked by the teacher.

3) What solutions they think may help them with either overcoming their inhibitions or with improving their speaking skills.

Teachers' questionnaire covers the same areas.

The survey

The first series of questions

Procedure: Students were given a situation: they are on holiday in the U.K. and want to call their friends up in Hungary. Their task is to go the reception desk and tell the receptionist the situation.

Analysis: Although it is not a difficult task, 90% oft he pupils answered that they would try to do so but they are not sure if they could tell what they want. Only are 4 % of the students certain that they can solve this problem.

It is surprising that similarly, 75% of the adult group felt the same and 25% found no difficulties in doing as indicated.

What can be the reason why students may not be able to fulfil such an easy situation? Teachers were asked whether they agreed the following or not: *'Children are taught plenty of grammar and vocabulary and they may be good at English, when they are in a real-life situation, they can not use the language properly or not dare to speak'.*

Most of the teachers say that students are lack of motivation and there is tiny little amount of time to explore the topics deeply as well as to revise because of the syllabus. The other problem is that it is not natural in Hungary for students to use and practise the target language outside the classroom. Not to mention that for most of the students, learning a foreign language is a boring process; they do not see how exciting it is to communicate in a foreign language, they just learn it because it is compulsory – suggested the teachers.

To get students accustomed to the target language it is very important to speak in it as many occasions as one can in the lessons. None of the teachers asked use the target language during the whole lesson. Most of them use it in 80-90% of the lesson.

Those who choose this percentage are satisfied with it because they consider it significant to explain the grammar in Hungarian so that everybody could understand it. According to the teachers, the indicated amount is enough also for developing the communication competence, even, mainly the lessons are the only opportunities for students to use the language.

While those who chose 80-90%, are between 30 and 50 years, it is very interesting that teachers between 20 and 30 use mother tongue half a lesson.

As for the question whether it is ideal or not, most of them were dissatisfied and gave the following reasons for the present situation:

- there is problem with students' basic knowledge
- students are this way deprived of the chance to practise or at least hear the target language
- there are too much subject material and little time for dealing with it, not to mention the bad division of the lessons
- if students' listening and writing skills were highly developed, more amount of the target language could be used

Second and third series of questions

Being a teacher, it is natural to go into the classroom, to hold the lesson, to give homework etc., and we do not think through what students may feel when being tested, for example, or just being questioned. It might not be as easy for them as we inclined to think.

45% of the students, mainly females, are always thinking whether they speak correctly or not while being asked.

In spite of the fact above, several of them indicate that they try to reply even if they are not sure. 25% say that in most of the cases they are able to express their thoughts. 10% are unsure in their knowledge and 11% are too shy to take risks and tell the answers despite that they know the correct ones. There is also a group of students who gave different reasons, for instance, they think on the question for too much time or the opposite, do not think, just say something. Others have problems with previous materials and there is a girl who says speaking is definitely an easy task and she enjoys it!

Thus, it should always be taken into consideration that students may feel embarrassed or have inhibitions and a teacher should be prepared for such cases. The following suggestions were given on behalf of the teachers questioned in the survey.

- the chief purpose is to make the student fell successful
- most of them would give easier exercise to those students
- pair or workgroup may help students become more brave
- more time is given to students for preparation

- keywords are on the board
- positive feedback: not correcting students' mistakes, only the very serious ones to make them get used to speaking
- explaining and expressing that they ARE allowed to make mistakes; creating a warm atmosphere
- to sit next to the student and encourage him or her
- trying to question every member of the group several times so that this way there is possibility for them to get used to speaking.

However, there might be cases when the last one is rather bad solution. The success of this idea is based on the personality of the better student. In case, s/he is ready to help without any prejudice, then this is fine but it should be overthought whether s/he will not abuse her/his position, which may paralyse the weaker one.

One of the teachers stated that her students seemed to be neutral rather than inhibited.

As far as the students concerned, they feel that involving more speaking exercise would help them to get rid of their inhibitions (37%), 35% think that more real-life situations should be dealt with during the lessons, and 22% would change the teacher's attitude to teaching. 6% considers forming drama class important as for losing their shyness.

There are two of them who found the alcohol and eating a sandwich the best solution.

In the third question, teachers were given some types of speaking tasks (role-play, language game, guessing, project and discussion) and they were expected to indicate how often they use them. It turned out that the most often used task is the role-play; language games and guessing are on the second place, and the project and the discussion are the less used ones.

According to the results, there are, however, teachers who sometimes use the last two, as well. Perhaps time is one of the causes. The preparation of a project work or a discussion is extremely time-consuming.

Any extra preparation also needs time but maybe it is worth dealing with the opportunities of using audio-visual aids, for example a photo can bring you closer to the students and vice versa, just mentioning one of the advantages.

It seems that pupils need these devices: they especially like photos, then word cards, drawings on the board. On the fourth place using a ball stands and it is surprising that more boys chose this than girls, who may not be expected from a 16-year-old boy. Pictures from newspapers are also popular but students do not really like writing on the board and the use of OHP.

Apart from the given equipment, they recommend the following aids as well: barchoba, learning funny expressions and slang, using cassette recorder, watching video films or short films and using computer. Some of them criticise the topic of the course book and would ask for more interesting ones.

Teachers seem to prefer pictures from newspapers, drawings on the board. They do not really intend to use photos and cards which students put into the first and second place. The use of video and balls is followed by the OHP, the usage of which both students and teachers are averse to. Teachers also suggest that storybooks, picture dictionary, supplementary materials photocopied from the teacher's book make the students more curious not to mention involving realias (maps, tickets, etc.).

An adult group was also asked about the use of visual aids. The group completely agreed that these means definitely assist their comprehension.

And they may help them relax: they come from work and it is very important to try to attract their attention and these aids can easily fulfil this task since they are very spectacular.

3.3. The effect of drama techniques concerning human factors: a role-play in the classroom. (An experiment)

'There is a disagreement among educators as to the value of Role Play in second language acquisition. (…) There is a general consensus that role play allows the students to use the target language in a meaningful way'.(Henderson,B., W.,2003: 88).

Using the target language meaningfully is one of the advantageous features of drama techniques. To be honest, meaningfulness and focusing of everyday situations in teaching are seldom present in foreign language classrooms these days in Hungary in spite of the fact that with this way of teaching people can learn how to express their feelings and first of all become aware of the layers of their personality besides studying a foreign language.

Secondly, the base of these techniques is 'playing' and the desire for playing is human nature. With the help of it , one can learn things faster and playing makes people relaxed, calm and not at least open. These three factors (relaxedness, calmness and openness) provide the best facilities inside students to be able to acquire the subject material.

Accordingly, drama may help both adults and children untie their inhibitions, i. e. drama is independent from ages. As the Hungarian educational system has followed the Prussian way of teaching, students may be surprised and worried when for example, a role-play is introduced for the first time in the lesson but by the end, they become relaxed.

Whether it is right in real life is the topic of the second part of the survey.

A role play

Procedure

Students are asked to invent and perform a story according to the following criteria:
- the story has to include four things: refusal, surprise, and kind of jump and kiss. There is no other restriction connected to the plot
- it depends on the students where and when the events take place and they are allowed to draw the characters, as well.
- The text of the story is only one sentence given by the teacher. Students in each role may exclusively use that certain sentence and nothing else. They are expected to use appropriate mime and intonation to express what they intend to make the audience understand.
- To make it clear when the play starts and ends, students are asked to say 'CURTAIN' in the beginning and at the end of their performance.

Orientation

Students are divided into small groups. The size of them varies between 5 to 7 members. In our case two classes did the same task: an adult group (aged from 18 to 40) and a teenage group (aged from 15 to 16).

In the former case, they were 7 (3:4) of them and the teenagers 15 (7:8) of them. The selection of the group members was random.

Activity

A. *Adult group*

'*Group A*':

In 'Group A' two males and a female student work together. During the preparation they needed no help. Their sentence, 'text' was: 'What do you want?'

Performance:

They put a chair in the middle of the classroom and the female student sat on it pretending to sleep. The two males 'were riding on a horse' next to her. They looked at the sleeping woman and asked each other: 'What do you want?' Then they agreed to *jump* off the horses. Both of them at same time gave a *kiss* to the woman on her cheeks. The woman woke up and asked *surprisedly*: 'What do you want?'. The men looked at each other, then at the woman, at each other again and in the end, they shot the woman as a *refusal*.

Note: it is a rather morbid way of expressing dislike but it should be acknowledged that the whole story is a creative one!

'*Group B*':

In 'Group B' there were three female and only one male students. They needed no help, either. Their sentence was: 'Oh, no!'

Performance:

Their story took place in the street. The three girls were just walking and suddenly a man *jumped* in front of them. He opened his coat. (He stood back the audience). The girls _refused_ him: 'Oh no!' The man got _surprised_ and tried to gain their approval: he threw _kisses_ towards the girls but they refused him again.

Analysis:

On the teacher's half: during the preparation and the performances, I felt that they enjoyed playing very much. It is true, however, that when I informed them about the exercise, they became worried a little bit: they have not taken part in such task.

On students' half: after the play students were asked to fill in a questionnaire about their feelings before, during and at the end of the task.

Listening to the instructions, 57% of them got surprised about it but they were looking forward to it. 29% said that they had different feelings out of the given ones but unfortunately they failed to indicate these.

During the play, 43% of the students felt embarrassed but by the end they enjoyed it. 29% felt nothing special about the task. The extremes are 14%: only one of them grew to like it from the beginning and one of them felt uneasy the duration of it.

As for the whole impression: 43% of them loved it and in the same proportion, students had worries in the beginning but also grew to like it by the end. Only one person (14%) refused it completely.

All in all, 86% (6 people) thought that role plays and situational role plays are useful.

B. Teenage group

'Group A':

'Group A' did not ask for help, they prepared for the performance completely on their own. Their sentence was: 'Please do it!'(See Appendix V).

Performance:

'Group A' took us to a classroom, to an English lesson. The teacher explained the material and then she has to leave. The students tried to beg her to stay but she _refused_ them, she left the room while students were throwing _kisses_ to her. One of the students wrote onto the board: 'One month later'. The teacher came back, the students were _surprised_ and started to _jump_ being informed by the good news.

'Group B':

In 'Group B' students were quite inadvisable so they need my help to a great extent. Their sentence was: 'What do you want?' (See Appendix V).

Performance:

We are on a birthday party. In the middle, there is the girl féted. Two other girls try to give her their birthday present but she *refuses* them saying: 'What do you want?'. The other girls are *surprised* and became very disappointed. On the left, there is a DJ (sitting next to a desk) and one of the girls tries to ask for a song. When it is on, she gets happy and runs and *jumps* to the others on the right and they dance together while trying to wake up the boy got exhausted by the party

Analysis:

On behalf of the teacher: they also became surprised as the adults but later there was no problem. The members of 'Group B' were a bit worried in the beginning, as they did not have ideas.

On behalf of the students:

According to the answers to the questionnaire: (See Appendix IV).

- Listening to the instructions, 73% of the students were looking forward to the task, 20% became anxious but later calm down. One person (7%) said that the task made him bored.
- During the play 53% enjoyed the game from the beginning to end. 20% worried first but by the end grew to like it and 20% had no special feelings about the play. It was unpleasant for only one person (7%).

As for the whole impression: 73% of the students spoke highly about the task, 13% had problems in the beginning but liked it on the whole. Two of them (14%) disliked it.

To sum up, 80% of the teenagers asked believe that these kinds of exercises are useful as they have chance to practise every day life-like situations in the target language. 13% say that this may be useful but they do not like them and one person (7%) consider role-play only a game, ineffective way of learning a language.

Conclusion

As the data of this brief survey suggest the majority of both the adolescents and the adults looked forward to such tasks and nearly the same percentage of them worried about it first.

It can be stated that youngsters may be rather ready to take risks, to undertake the new than the older ones. (Teenagers who enjoyed the game from the beginning: 53% while adults: 14%).

Adults seem to need more time to be used to the unknown situation: adults who worried in the beginning: 43% while children: 20%. According to the answers for question 3.3, 73% of pupils liked the task very much. It is very interesting that as for the adult group the rate is 43% for the category mentioned above and it is the same as the one's who needed time to let themselves go.

All in all, it can be declared that by this role play the majority of the people managed to get rid of the paralysing factors: they became relaxed and opened even if they may have been anxious about the unknown task.

The teachers were also questioned whether they used drama techniques or not. 54% of them uses the method exclusively as the completion of course books, 38% does not know the techniques thoroughly, therefore, avoid introducing it. Only one person (8%) believes in it and organises drama classes, as well.

Final remarks

This work is an attempt to give a brief summary of the up-tp date methods of teaching speaking looking also back in the historical facts.

There may be various attitudes to teaching but it may be agreed on that without creating an atmosphere in which both the teacher and the students feel at home, teaching loses its effectiveness, no matter which skill is in question.

Although children may be under-motivated nowadays as plenty of teachers I have talked to suggested but making them involved in the learning process should not be given for the first try. Most of the children are rather neglected today and that is why does count for them what a teacher says.

As for students' improvement in speaking, it is apparent from the survey that students would need more practice but it can not be fulfilled because of the quantity of the subject material specified for a school year.

Thus, it revealed that the most urgent problems are the question of time and probably, the requirements of students would be worth thinking over, as well.

It is a usual process that students start learning a language in the first years of primary school then carries it on in the grammar school. The majority of them are even unable to pass a state examination of intermediate level nevertheless, they had been learning the target language for at least 9 years! From the above facts it is clear to see that reforms should be done in the future. Part of the change might as well be the use drama techniques as it turned out that only few teachers know the method thoroughly. What is significant at this point, however, is that students should also be asked. Language learning should always depend on the needs of the students and it may be a great challenge for teachers, too.

All in all, it is not easy to train students, firstly, to use their common sense, and secondly, to make them enable to use the target language in reality when the educational system is based on theoretical knowledge.

In spite of these, by a consistent teaching behaviour the devices having been discussed may prove to be one of the solutions to this problem.

Appendices

Appendix I.

Table 1.

A comparison of anxious and good learners

Anxious learner	Good learner (Wenden, Rubin, 1987)
Is reluctant to take risks (Ely, 1986)	Is willing to take risks
Relies heavily on memory	Is tolerant of ambiguities
Is reluctant to hypothesize (Mac Intryre and Gardner, 1994)	Possesses good cognitive strategies of guessing and inferring
Is disorganised and inefficient in recall of learned items (Mac Intyre and Gardner, 1994)	Shows good strategies of monitoring, categorizing and synthetising
Feels apprehension and self-doubts, is frustrated (Arnold and Brown, 1999)	Shows positive attitude, is sociable and outgoing

Source: Turula, Anna, Language Anxiety and Classroom Dynamics: A Study of Adult Learners, 40, 2002, p. 28-33, 31.

Appendix II.

Picture 1.

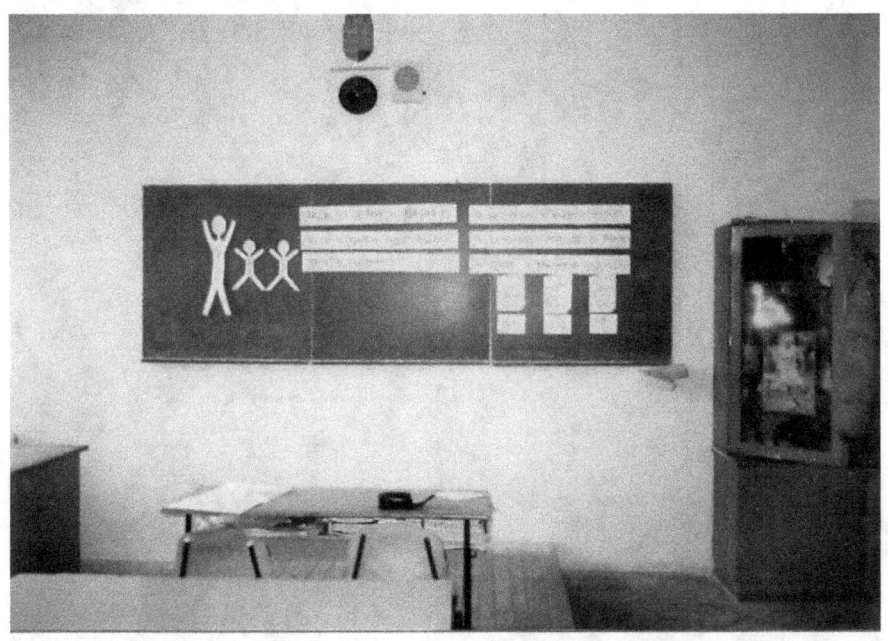

Paper figures for explaining the comparison of adjectives

Appendix III.

Picture II/a
Pairwork: students are choosing a partner with the help of ribbons.

Picture II/b.
Working in '…small groups provide greater intensity of involvement…'
(Brumfit, 1994)

Appendix IV.

Questionnaire for the survey/ students

(The people involved in this survey were asked in their mother tongue. This is a translation of the original questionnaire.)

Your sex:
Your age:

1. **Imagine that you are abroad on a holiday. You are staying at a hotel and you would like to phone your friends at home. You can use the telephone at the reception desk, so you have to go there and say what you want in English. (In your family you are the only person who speaks English). Would it be a problem for you to do so? Tick the anwer you feel the best for you.**

    a) I wouldn't dare to go there and speak in English despite of the fact that I have learnt some expressions involved in such situations
    b) I would try it but I am not sure that I managed to say what I want.
    c) I wouldn't dare to go there, I always feel embarrassed in such situations.
    d) Other:

2. **Choose the realias which you think useful and like the best as supplementary materials in an English lesson:**
    a) Pictures cut from newspapers and magazines
    b) Using OHP
       drawings on the board
    c) If you are allowed and asked to write on the board
    d) Using a ball
    e) Using cards with words on them
    f) Other:

3. **When the teacher asks you something,**

A) it is always difficult for me to speak because
    a) I am not confident and I am not talkative, anyway.
    b) Most of the cases I know the answer but I don't dare to talk
    c) While speaking I always keep thinking of whether I make a mistake or not
    d) Other:

B) It is not difficult for me to talk in English because
    a) I say the anwer even if I am not sure in it.
    b) I usually know the answer and it isn't difficult for me to express my opinion.
    c) Other:

4. **According to your view**

A) what can help you get rid of your inhibitions?
   a) The attitude of the teacher
   b) More practice of speech
   c) A drama circle in English
   d) More everyday life situations in the lessons
   e) Other:

B) how can you improve your speaking skills?

   a) with a change in the attitude of the teacher
   b) more speaking practice
   c) English drama circle
   d) More everyday life situations in the lessons

5. Have you ever taken part into a Hungarian drama circle?

If yes, would you like to try it in English as well?

   a) I would feel like to do so, but I am afraid that my English is not good enough
   b) Sure, I consider it an excellent idea

If no, why not?
   a) I am not interested in such things.
   b) I would be interested in it but I haven't been brave enough to have a try.

Thank you for your cooperation!

2. Questinnaire for the survey/teachers

Your sex:
Your age:
The course-books you use:

1. **Do you agree with the following statement?**

' Children learn a lot in the English lessons but when they get into an everyday life situation, such a shopping, they are unable to use what they have learnt'

If you agree with this statements, what can the reasons be behind this phenomenon?
   a) The educational system is not good enough
   b) There is only little time to deal with certain topics because of the requirements
   c) The course-book in use is not suitable
   d) Students are under-motivated
   e) Other:

In case you disagree, please give reasons.
....
....
....

2. **In what percentage do you speak in English in your lessons?**
   a) 100%
   b) 90-80 %
   c) 50%
   d) 20-30%
   e) 0%

3. **In your opinion, is this percentage suitable? Give reasons both for and against.**
....
....
....

4. **How often do you use the following tasks in your lessons?**
   a) Role play
   b) Language games
   c) Guessing
   d) Project work
   e) Discussions
   f) Other:

5. **What realias do you use?**

   a) Pictures cut from newspapers and magazines
   b) Using OHP
      drawings on the board
   c) If you are allowed and asked to write on the board
   d) Using a ball

e) Using cards with words on them
   f) English-speaking films
   g) Other:

How often do you use the realias mentioned above?
   a) Whenever I can, I use them
   b) Rarely, I don't have too much time for their preparation
   c) I don't use such things at all

6. There are a lot of reasons why a student does not dare to speak in English. When you realize that your student is shy, how do you usually help him/her?

7. Are you interested in drama pedagogy?

If yes, which field of drama do you use?
   a) I use it only in my lessons
   b) I really appreciate this method, I organize drama circles
   c) Other:

If not, why?
   a) I do not know much about this method
   b) I have seen such tasks before but I did not like it
   c) Other:

ATTENTION! THE LAST QUESTION SHOULD BE ANSWERED IF YOU SAY YES IN QUESTION 7 !

8. Involving drama in your work, what changes on children could you realize?
   a) Some of them enjoyed it from the beginning
   b) Some of them disliked it at first but they soon get to like it
   c) Some of them hated it from the beginning.
   d) Other:

Thank you for answering. Wish you all the best!

3. Questionnaire for the survey/experiment

Your age:
Your sex:

Think of a role-play you have been involved, please.

Before the role-play

   a) How did you feel when you were told that a role-play was coming?
   b) I was surprised and it made me feel embarrassed
   c) I was surprised and it made me feel embarrassed but when it was clear for me what the task is exactly, I calmed down
   d) I was surprised but I am open-minded so I was looking forward to it

During the role-play

How did you feel during the role-play?
   a) I enjoyed it from the beginning
   b) I was tense at the beginning but in the end I enjoyed it
   c) It was frightening for me from the beginning, I felt as if I was naked.
   d) I did not feel anything special, it was only a task to do

Your impressions on drama technique

All in all, what do you think of this method?
   a) I really liked it!
   b) I like it but just in the end.
   c) I really hated it
   d) Other:

What is your opinion about role-plays and situational plays as methods of learning and teaching English?

   a) It is a very good way to learn English because while playing different games we practise the language
   b) It may be useful but I disliked it
   c) It is just a game
   d) Other:

Thank you for your answer.

Appendix V.

Picture V./a
Teenage group A acting out the role-play.

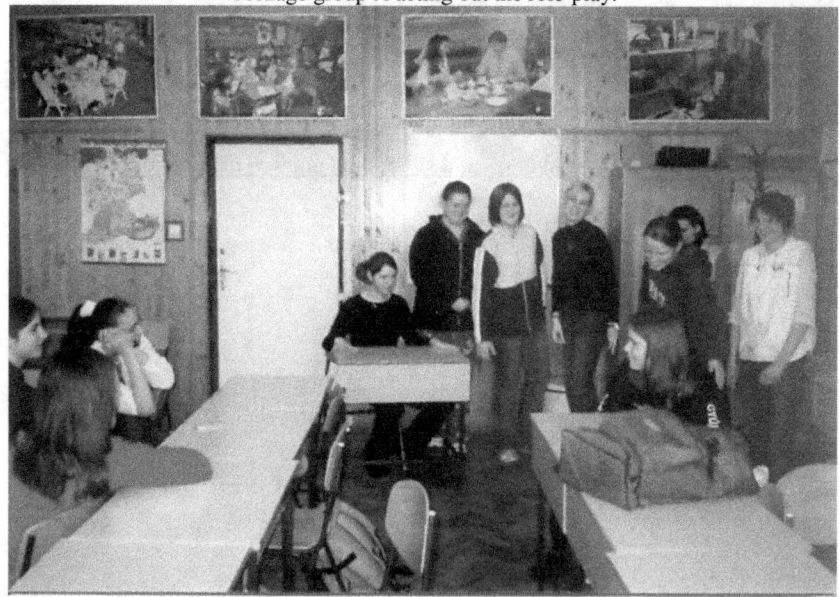

Picture V.b
Teenage group B acting out the role-play.

Appendix VI.

The effect of drama techniques concerning human factors

An experiment

The results of the questionnarire

Numbers of the questions		Answers in percentage Teens / Adults	
3. 1	a)	-	-
	b)	20	14
	c)	73	57
	Other	7	29
3.2	a)	53	14
	b)	20	43
	c)	7	14
	d)	20	29
	Other	-	-
3.3	a)	73	43
	b)	13	43
	c)	7	14
	Other	7	-
3.4	a)	80	86
	b)	13	14
	c)	7	-
	Other	-	-

Works consulted

Bárdos Jenő, Az idegennyelvek tanításának elméleti alapjai, Nemzeti Tankönyvkiadó, Budapest, 2000.

Bárdos Jenő, Nyelvtanítás: múlt és jelen, Magvető Kiadó, Budapest, 1988.

Bárdos Jenő, A nyelvtanítás története és a módszertanfogalom tartalma, Veszprémi Egyetemi Kiadó, 1997.

Bandains, Richard and Marjorine, Alternatives, Longman, 1989.

Bygate, Martin, Speaking, Oxford University Press, 1987.

Csoma Katalin, Thoughts on Humanist Curriculum Theorising, Novelty, 10, 2003, pp 58-65.

Gabnai Katalin, Drámajátékok, Marczibányi Téri Művelődési Központ, Budapest, 1993.

Gower, Roger, Diane Philips, Steve Heinemann, Teaching Practice Handbook, Great Britain, 1995.

Henderson, William, Learners as jurors in the second language classroom: a role-play, Novelty, 10, 2003, pp. 86-90.

Kurtán Zsuzsa, Linguistics and the English language, Veszprémi Egyetemi Kiadó, Veszprém, 1999.

Ladousse, Gillian Porter, Role Play, Oxford University Press, Oxford.

Maley, Allan, Drama, Oxford University Press, Oxford, 1987.

McAlpin, Janet, The Magazine Picture Library, George Allan and Unwin Ltd, London, 1980

Poór Zoltán, A kommunikatív szemlélet megvalósulási formái a gyermekkori nyelvtanításban, Kecskeméti Tanárképző Főiskola Kiadója, Kecskemét, 1995.

Poór Zoltán, Nyelvpedagógiai technológia, Nemzeti Tankönyvkiadó, Budapest, 2001.

Takács Lajos, Neveléstörténet, Veszprémi Egyetemi Kiadó, Veszprém, 1996.

Turula, Anna, Language anxiety and classroom dynamics – A study of adult learners, Novelty, 40, 2002, pp 28-33.

www.ingramcontent.com/pod-product-compliance
Lightning Source LLC
Chambersburg PA
CBHW071416290426
44108CB00014B/1849